## This journal belongs to

_____

AN AQUARIAN EXPOSITION:

# 3 DAYS OF PEACE & MUSIC

August 15, 16, and 17, 1969. Woodstock Music & Art Fair organizers expected 50,000 attendees. They'd had trouble securing a venue until dairy farmer Max Yasgur agreed to let them use his 600-acre farm in Bethel, New York. Until April, they'd also had trouble signing popular performers. But when the festival began, more than 400,000 attendees arrived. By the time it ended, 32 of the most iconic rock and folk acts of the 1960s had taken the stage. They played in the sun, the rain, and the middle of the night. Rock & roll legends were created, a generation was defined, and music was changed forever.

**FRIDAY**

| | |
|---|---|
| 5:07 | Richie Havens |
| 7:10 | invocation from Swami Satchidananda |
| 7:30 | Sweetwater |
| 8:20 | Bert Sommer |
| 9:20 | Tim Hardin |
| 10:00 | Ravi Shankar |
| 10:50 | Melanie |
| 11:55 | Arlo Guthrie |
| 12:55 | Joan Baez |

**SATURDAY**

| | |
|---|---|
| 12:15 | Quill |
| 1:00 | Country Joe McDonald |
| 2:00 | Santana |
| 3:30 | John Sebastian |
| 4:45 | Keef Hartley Band |
| 6:00 | The Incredible String Band |
| 7:30 | Canned Heat |
| 9:00 | Mountain |
| 10:30 | Grateful Dead |
| 12:30 | Creedence Clearwater Revival |
| 2:00 | Janis Joplin with the Kozmic Blues Band |
| 3:30 | Sly and the Family Stone |
| 5:00 | The Who |
| 8:00 | Jefferson Airplane |

**SUNDAY**

| | |
|---|---|
| 2:00 | Joe Cocker and the Grease Band |
| 6:30 | Country Joe and the Fish |
| 8:15 | Ten Years After |
| 10:00 | The Band |
| 12:00 | Johnny Winter |
| 1:30 | Blood, Sweat & Tears |
| 3:00 | Crosby, Stills, Nash & Young |
| 6:00 | Paul Butterfield Blues Band |
| 7:30 | Sha Na Na |
| 9:00 | Jimi Hendrix/Gypsy Sun & Rainbows |

"I SAY, FOLLOW YOUR BLISS AND DON'T BE AFRAID, AND DOORS WILL OPEN WHERE YOU DIDN'T KNOW THEY WERE GOING TO BE."

—Joseph Campbell

* PEACE * LOVE * MUSIC * PEACE * LOVE

* PEACE * LOVE * MUSIC * PEACE * LOVE

FLOWER POWER ✿ FLOWER POWER ✿ FLOWER POWER ✿ FLOWER POWER ✿ FLOWER POWER

"I'M NOT WORRIED ABOUT THE SECURITY PARTICULARLY. IF PEOPLE HAVE ENOUGH TO DO, THERE WON'T BE TROUBLE."

—WESLEY A. POMEROY, HEAD OF SECURITY AT WOODSTOCK

* PEACE * LOVE * MUSIC * PEACE * LOVE

* PEACE * LOVE * MUSIC * PEACE * LOVE

FLOWER POWER ✿ FLOWER POWER ✿ FLOWER POWER ✿ FLOWER POWER ✿ FLOWER POWER

"[IN THE 1960s] WE WERE YOUNG, WE WERE RECKLESS, ARROGANT, SILLY, HEAD-STRONG ... AND WE WERE RIGHT! I REGRET NOTHING!"

—ABBIE HOFFMAN

PEACE * LOVE * MUSIC * PEACE * LOVE * M

PEACE * LOVE * MUSIC * PEACE * LOVE * N

* PEACE * LOVE * MUSIC * PEACE * LOVE

* PEACE * LOVE * MUSIC * PEACE * LOVE

FLOWER POWER ❁ FLOWER POWER ❁ FLOWER POWER ❁ FLOWER POWER ❁ FLOWER POWER

"THINK FOR YOURSELF AND QUESTION AUTHORITY."

—TIMOTHY LEARY

* PEACE * LOVE * MUSIC * PEACE * LOVE

* PEACE * LOVE * MUSIC * PEACE * LOVE

FLOWER POWER ❀ FLOWER POWER ❀ FLOWER POWER ❀ FLOWER POWER ❀ FLOWER POWER

"PEACE CAN BE MADE ONLY BY THOSE WHO ARE PEACEFUL,
AND LOVE CAN BE SHOWN ONLY BY THOSE WHO LOVE."

—ALAN WATTS

\* PEACE \* LOVE \* MUSIC \* PEACE \* LOVE

\* PEACE \* LOVE \* MUSIC \* PEACE \* LOVE

FLOWER POWER ✿ FLOWER POWER ✿ FLOWER POWER ✿ FLOWER POWER ✿ FLOWER POWER

"LIKE WOW, THESE PEOPLE ARE REALLY BEAUTIFUL, THE COPS, THE STOREKEEPERS, THE ARMY, EVERYBODY."

—Laura Glazer, a Woodstock attendee

* PEACE * LOVE * MUSIC * PEACE * LOVE

* PEACE * LOVE * MUSIC * PEACE * LOVE

FLOWER POWER ❀ FLOWER POWER ❀ FLOWER POWER ❀ FLOWER POWER ❀ FLOWER POWER

"DON'T BOTHER MAX'S COWS. LET THEM MOO IN PEACE."

—SIGN AT **WOODSTOCK**

* PEACE * LOVE * MUSIC * PEACE * LOVE

* PEACE * LOVE * MUSIC * PEACE * LOVE

FLOWER POWER ❀ FLOWER POWER ❀ FLOWER POWER

FLOWER POWER ❀ FLOWER POWER ❀ FLOWER POWER

"GOOD MORNING! WHAT WE HAVE IN MIND IS
BREAKFAST IN BED FOR 400,000."

—WAVY GRAVY, SPEAKING FROM THE STAGE

* PEACE * LOVE * MUSIC * PEACE * LOVE

* PEACE * LOVE * MUSIC * PEACE * LOVE

FLOWER POWER ❀ FLOWER POWER ❀ FLOWER POWER ❀ FLOWER POWER ❀ FLOWER POWER

"THE WHOLE THING IS A GAS. I DIG IT ALL,
THE MUD, THE RAIN, THE MUSIC, THE HASSLES."

—SPEED, A WOODSTOCK ATTENDEE

FLOWER POWER ❁ FLOWER POWER ❁ FLOWER POWER ❁ FLOWER POWER ❁ FLOWER POWER

"THE IMPORTANT THING THAT YOU'VE PROVEN TO THE WORLD IS THAT A HALF A MILLION KIDS—AND I CALL YOU KIDS BECAUSE I HAVE CHILDREN THAT ARE OLDER THAN YOU—A HALF MILLION YOUNG PEOPLE CAN GET TOGETHER AND HAVE THREE DAYS OF FUN AND MUSIC AND HAVE NOTHING BUT FUN AND MUSIC, AND I GOD BLESS YOU FOR IT!"

—MAX YASGUR

\* PEACE \* LOVE \* MUSIC \* PEACE \* LOVE

\* PEACE \* LOVE \* MUSIC \* PEACE \* LOVE

FLOWER POWER ❀ FLOWER POWER ❀ FLOWER POWER ❀ FLOWER POWER ❀ FLOWER POWER

ISBN 978-1-64178-023-0

We are always looking for talented authors and artists. To submit an idea, please send a brief inquiry to acquisitions@foxchapelpublishing.com.

Printed in China
First printing